AMERICA'S ETHNIC DIVERSITY

LATIN AMERICANS

by Johannah Luza

BrightPoint Press

San Diego, CA

an imprint of ReferencePoint Press, Inc.
Printed in the United States

For more information, contact:
BrightPoint Press
PO Box 27779
San Diego, CA 92198
www.BrightPointPress.com

LIBRARY OF CONGRESS CATALOGING-IN-PUBLICATION DATA

Name: Luza, Johannah, author.
Title: Latin Americans / by Johannah Luza.
Description: San Diego, CA: ReferencePoint Press, 2026 | Series: America's Ethnic Diversity | Audience: Grade 7 to 9 | Includes bibliographical references and index.
Identifiers: ISBN: 9781678211042 (hardcover) | ISBN: 9781678211059 (eBook)
The complete Library of Congress record is available at www.loc.gov.

CONTENTS

AT A GLANCE

- In the 1400s and 1500s, Spanish and Portuguese explorers colonized parts of Central and South America. Over time, their languages and cultures spread across Mexico and South America. They mixed with Indigenous languages and cultures.

- Latin Americans are people of Mexican, Central American, South American, or Caribbean origin.

- The first influx of Latin Americans to the United States took place after the Mexican-American War (1846–1848). This was fought over the US–Texas boundary. Mexico lost the war and gave up territory, including land that later became several US states.

- Latin Americans have made major contributions to the country. During World War II (1939–1945), many Latin Americans enlisted in the US military. Others filled jobs that white soldiers left behind.

- Latin Americans have rich, diverse cultures. They have contributed to US politics, sports, and entertainment. They have also introduced languages, holidays, and popular foods.

- Today, most Latin Americans are Catholic or Protestant. Some are Jewish. Some Latin Americans celebrate religious holidays, such as Las Posadas.

- In 2023, there were about 65.2 million Latin Americans in the United States.

- Immigration over the US–Mexico border has become a major issue in the United States. Political parties are divided on how to solve the problem.

THE QUINCEAÑERA

Miranda was excited. The day had finally come for her quinceañera. This is a **rite** of passage. It is part of many Latin American cultures. It marks a girl's fifteenth birthday. In the past, a quinceañera meant a girl was ready for marriage. Today, it has evolved. It means a girl is ready to date.

More than 500,000 quinceañeras take place in the United States every year. Most are in Florida, Texas, and California.

Girls usually wear special ball gowns for their quinceañeras. These dresses come in many styles and colors. Some girls also wear tiaras and carry bouquets.

But the tradition has caught on in every state.

Miranda and her family had been planning her quinceañera for months. Miranda's cousins were coming. They were from Mexico City, Mexico. They had traveled to Texas for the celebration. They would be part of Miranda's "court of *damas*," or maids of honor. Miranda had also invited her two best friends. Their names were Amy and Madison. They had never been to a quinceañera before. Miranda could not wait for them to see her royal-blue gown. She was also planning to wear a tiara. Her aunt had given it to her.

The celebration began with a **mass**. It took place at a Catholic church. After the mass, the party started. It was held

At many quinceañera receptions, the first dance is a father-daughter dance.

in a ballroom. Many aunts, uncles, and cousins were there. Everyone was looking at Miranda. She spotted Amy and Madison. They looked a little nervous. Miranda walked over and hugged them. "Wow," said Amy. "This is like a wedding!"

Soon, music began to play. Everyone watched Miranda and her father. They danced a waltz. Then Miranda and her court performed a dance. They had practiced it for weeks. Before long, everyone was dancing and laughing.

Later, dinner was served. Miranda stood up to speak. So did her younger sister, Bella. Miranda picked up a doll. She had gotten it for her sixth birthday. She handed the doll to Bella. This act symbolized that Miranda was giving up her childhood. Then Miranda's uncle gave a speech. It was in Spanish. After dinner, the partygoers enjoyed more music and dancing.

A RICH CULTURE

Quinceañeras are just one of many traditions that Latin Americans celebrate. Latin American cultures are rich and diverse. *Latin American* describes a person of Latin American **origin**. This includes people with Mexican origin. It also includes those with Central American, South American, or Caribbean origin.

Many Latin American **immigrants** have come to the United States. They do so for different reasons. Throughout history, Latin

Latin Americans may celebrate their cultures by sharing traditional foods.

In many cities throughout the United States, people hold parades and festivals to celebrate Latin American cultures and traditions.

Americans have influenced many areas of US culture. They have introduced traditional foods and music. They have also influenced business, sports, and politics.

The many thousands of Latin Americans in the United States have helped shape the country. Today, the United States is home to diverse ethnic groups. Diversity means having groups of people with different ethnic backgrounds. This includes religion, culture, and race. Diversity is what makes up the fabric of the United States. It strengthens communities. It brings a mix of unique people together.

CHAPTER ONE

THE HISTORY OF LATIN AMERICANS

Latin American culture in the United States has a long history. It dates back to before the country was established. In the late 1400s, Spanish colonists arrived in the Americas. Indigenous peoples had long lived there. But the Spanish took over the lands of Indigenous peoples. These included the Aztec people. They also included the Pueblo and Maya peoples.

Spanish explorer Juan Ponce de León is recognized as the first European to reach what is now Florida. A statue of him stands at a site in Melbourne Beach, Florida.

EARLY EXPLORERS

Early Spanish and Portuguese explorers colonized parts of Central and South America. Throughout the 1400s and 1500s, they spread across the continents. The Europeans forced Indigenous peoples off their homelands. They brought diseases. Many Indigenous people died from these diseases. European settlers also established churches called missions. Missions worked to convert Indigenous peoples to Christianity. Missionaries forced them to adopt Christian ways of life.

Over time, Spanish language and culture spread. They spread from Mexico to the southernmost part of South America. They mixed with many different Indigenous languages and cultures. Eventually, Spanish and Portuguese became main languages in these areas. The region became known as Latin America. This is because both languages come from Latin.

Some explorers claimed US territories for Spain. Some would later become US states. These included Texas, New Mexico, and Arizona. California and Florida were

Spanish and Portuguese settlers established many missions throughout Central and South America. They sought to convert Indigenous peoples to Christianity.

included, too. Over the next two centuries, more Spanish people settled in these areas.

THE FIRST LATIN AMERICANS

The first influx of Latin Americans to the United States happened in the 1800s. It took place after the Mexican American War (1846–1848). Mexico fought the United States in this war. They fought over the US–Texas boundary. Mexico didn't recognize Texas as a US territory. But in 1845, Texas was named a US state. This angered Mexican officials and citizens.

Mexico lost the war. It had to give up land to the United States. Mexico lost 55 percent of its territory. This included what are now California, Nevada, Utah, and Arizona. It also included New Mexico, Colorado, and Texas. Parts of Oklahoma, Kansas, and Wyoming were included, too. Mexico and the United States agreed to a peace treaty in 1848. It was called the Treaty of Guadalupe Hidalgo. It offered US citizenship to thousands of former Mexican citizens. These citizens were living north of the border when the war ended.

The 1847 Battle of Chapultepec was a major battle in the Mexican-American War. During the battle, US forces stormed a castle in Mexico City, Mexico.

Many people from Mexico and Chile came to California during the California Gold Rush.

CALIFORNIA GOLD RUSH

Soon after the treaty was signed, people heard that gold had been discovered. People found it in California. Hundreds of Chileans and Mexicans traveled to California mining camps. They joined Spanish-speaking Californians there. By 1850, many English-speaking Americans had become upset. They thought Latinos were taking their jobs. English-speaking Americans started driving Latin Americans out of California. This was a form of racism. In the following decades, California's Latin American population grew slowly.

In the 1900s, the United States grew fast. In 1917, Woodrow Wilson was president. He declared Puerto Rico a US territory. This granted citizenship to all Puerto Ricans.

Meanwhile, workers were needed to extend railroad tracks. Tracks stretched from eastern cities to the western frontier. Settlers were starting to farm land, too. People of Mexican **heritage** came to the United States to work. By 1930, more than 1.6 million people of Mexican heritage lived there. But in the 1930s, an economic slump happened. Many people lost their jobs. Some white Americans blamed Latin American workers. White Americans thought Latinos were taking their jobs. US policies forced thousands of Mexican Americans to return to Mexico. This included workers who had come to the United States. It also included Mexican Americans who had been born in the United States.

WORLD WAR II AND BEYOND

In 1941, the United States became involved in World War II (1939–1945). This war started when Nazi Germany invaded Poland. The United States allied with the United Kingdom and France. The Soviet Union joined them. Together, they fought Germany, Japan, and Italy. Many American workers joined US troops. The US government needed workers to fill the

In 1942, the US government started a guest worker program known as the Bracero Program. Many Mexican American workers who participated took jobs on farms.

jobs they left behind. They started a guest worker program with Mexico. It brought thousands of Mexicans back to the United States. Some worked in factories. Others worked on farms.

But 350,000 Mexican Americans also joined the military. About 53,000 Puerto Ricans joined, too. These Latin Americans were proud to serve the United States. General Douglas MacArthur was a military commander. He was impressed by one of the Latino and Native American combat units. He said, "No greater fighting combat team has ever deployed for battle."[1]

For years, immigration to the United States was not **regulated**. After the war, that changed. White American soldiers returned home. They needed jobs. So between 1954 and 1955, the US government held a mass deportation. It deported Mexicans who had entered the country illegally.

Immigration laws were tightened in the 1960s. In 1965, the Immigration and Nationality Act passed. It set new rules for temporary worker visas. These allowed foreign citizens to enter the United States. There, they could work for a certain time period. Under the act, only a limited number

Zoot Suit Riots

During World War II, many Latin American youths wore long dress coats. They wore these with baggy pants. These were called zoot suits. Some Latin American youths in Los Angeles, California, formed gangs. They wore zoot suits. Many white people began associating zoot suits with gangs. But many people who wore them were not in gangs. Servicemen often assumed zoot suiters were draft dodgers. In 1943, riots broke out. Sailors and zoot suiters got into a fight. People began seeking out and beating Latin Americans.

COUNTRIES IN LATIN AMERICA

Latin America includes many different countries. Immigrants have come to the United States from these countries.

of Mexican workers could receive visas. But the new law also abolished quotas that favored only European immigrants. This led to an increase in immigration from Asian and Latin American countries. For some Latin Americans, the immigration process became easier. But the Act's limits made it harder for other Latin Americans.

Today, Latin Americans still immigrate to the United States for many reasons. Some want to escape poverty or crime. They want their children to have a better education. Others want to live in a country that is not ruled by dictators. Many are willing to take risks to come to the United States. In 1990, there were 21 million Latin Americans in the country. By 2017, that number had grown to 58 million.

CHAPTER TWO

CULTURES AND TRADITIONS

Latin Americans have rich cultures and traditions. Their cultures are diverse. Latin American traditions differ depending on geography and heritage. Throughout history, Latinos have worked to share and protect these traditions. They have helped shape American society in many ways.

One contribution is language. Most Latin Americans speak Spanish. Spanish is the second-most-spoken language in

Many Latin Americans celebrate their culture through traditional music and art forms.

YORK

the United States. More than 40 million people in the United States speak Spanish at home. In 2022, more than 10 million students were learning Spanish in schools. The language is taught in elementary, middle, and high schools. Many US families speak both English and Spanish.

Family is also part of Latin American culture. In the past, it was common for three generations to live together. This is still true for some Latin American families. Grandparents play an important role in many families. They help raise children.

TRADITIONAL DISHES

Food is a huge part of Latin American culture. It is seen as something that brings families together. Latin American food has

Popular Mexican and Tex-Mex dishes include tacos, nachos, refried beans, and enchiladas.

long been popular in the United States. One example is Tex-Mex food. This is a blend of Texan and Mexican cuisine. It is not as spicy as authentic Mexican food. Fajitas are one famous Tex-Mex dish.

One popular Peruvian dish is ceviche. This is white fish soaked in citrus juice. It is spiced with chili peppers, onions, and cilantro. Cuban sandwiches are another Latin American food. South Florida is known for these. The sandwiches are filled with ham, pickles, mustard, and Swiss cheese.

Latin American desserts have made their way to the United States, too. One is dulce de leche. In Spanish, this means "sweet made from milk." It is similar to caramel. It is made with milk and sugar. Dulce de leche is often used as a dessert topping or filling. Flan is a custard-like dish. It is sometimes filled with dulce de leche.

HOLIDAYS

Latin Americans celebrate many holidays. One is Cinco de Mayo. In Spanish, Cinco de Mayo means "May 5." On this day in 1862, Mexico declared victory over France.

France had invaded Mexico. It said Mexico owed it money. On Cinco de Mayo, people celebrate Mexico's victory. They throw parties. They eat Mexican food. In May 2023, President Joe Biden said, "Cinco de Mayo is a day to celebrate the **resilience**, culture, and heritage of generations of Mexican Americans."[2]

National Hispanic Heritage Month

Many Americans observe National Hispanic Heritage Month. It lasts from September 15 to October 15. It celebrates the cultures of Hispanic Americans. These are people with backgrounds in Spain, Mexico, the Caribbean, and Central and South America. The honor started in 1968 as Hispanic Heritage Week. In 1988, it changed to a month. During this time, people hold festivals. Concerts, parades, and events take place.

Many Latin Americans celebrate Día de los Muertos by setting up altars, or *ofrendas*. These are often decorated with marigolds, candles, and pictures of loved ones.

Another Latin American holiday is Día de los Muertos. In Spanish, this means "Day of Dead." It takes place on November 1 and 2. On this holiday, Latin Americans honor loved ones who have died. People often decorate graves with candles. They build altars in their homes. These honor the souls of the dead. People place pictures and items that belonged to their relatives at the altars. They place flowers and candles there, too. People also make skulls out of sugar. They paint them to honor their relatives. For Latin Americans, Día de los Muertos is not a sad or gloomy occasion. It is a day to remember good times and honor loved ones.

One big Latin American celebration takes place in Miami, Florida. It is called Calle Ocho. It is one of the biggest block parties in the world. In Spanish, Calle Ocho means "Eighth Street." People worldwide come to see the nation's largest Latin American music festival. It is held in a

Cuban neighborhood. It is part of Carnival Miami. Carnival is a holiday common in Latin America. It takes place before Lent. This is a season observed by Christians. Carnival involves parades and music. Millie Garcia attended Calle Ocho in 2023. She said, "The food, the music, the dance, the people! I think that's the best part."[3]

Birthdays are also big celebrations in Latin American communities. One traditional birthday food is tres leches cake. It is made with three milks. Many birthday celebrations feature a piñata, too. This is a papier-mâché container. It is sometimes shaped like an animal or cartoon character. The piñata is hung high. Then children take turns hitting it with a stick. When the piñata breaks open, candy and fruit spill out.

The annual Calle Ocho Music Festival features live dance and music performances. Visitors can also enjoy food and crafts.

CHAPTER THREE

RELIGIONS

Most Latin Americans in the United States are Catholic. But in 2022, those numbers were declining. The second-largest religion among Latin Americans is Protestant. Young Latin Americans born in the United States are more likely to not belong to any religious branch.

A 2023 survey asked young Latin Americans about their religions. Some said

For many Latino Catholics in the United States, Our Lady of Guadalupe is an important religious figure. She represents Mary, the mother of Jesus.

REINA DE MEXICO Y
EMPERATRIZ DE AMERICA

they stopped believing in their childhood religion. Others found a different religion. Nine percent of those who changed faiths married someone of a different religion.

A small number of Spanish Americans are Jewish. Jews with roots in Spain or Portugal are called Sephardic Jews. Today, about 250,000 to 300,000 Sephardic Jews live in the United States.

In 1492, Spain had a large population of Jews. Queen Isabella and King Ferdinand ruled Spain. They were Catholic. They ordered Jews to convert to Catholicism. If they refused, they would have to leave Spain. Some people did not convert but secretly kept their Jewish faith. Many other Jews left Spain. Some immigrated to Central and South America.

RELIGIOUS HOLIDAYS

For many Latin Americans, the week before Easter is a holy week. It is called Semana Santa. Every year during this week, thousands of people gather. They walk to Santuario de Chimayo. This church is in New Mexico. The walk is the largest ritual **pilgrimage** in the United States. "In coming to Chimayo, people participate

For many Catholics, the pilgrimage to Chimayo is a time for healing and reflection. The trek represents Jesus's journey to the cross in the Christian Bible.

in Christ's journey to [his crucifixion site]," explains a priest.[4] Some people walk more than 70 miles (113 km) from Albuquerque, New Mexico.

People often carry homemade crosses as they walk. Some crosses are 8 feet (2.4 m) tall. The pilgrims wait for hours to

The Legend of Chimayo

There is a legend about Chimayo. It takes place in the 1800s. A man found a cross buried at Chimayo. He took it to his church. But then the cross vanished. It was found again at Chimayo. The townspeople decided to build a church there. It was completed in 1815. Today, people who journey to Chimayo go to a small chapel. It is near the sanctuary. Only two or three people can enter the chapel at a time. The floor has an open pit of earth. It is said to have healing powers. Some people gather the dirt in plastic bags.

enter the adobe chapel. They leave notes of thanksgiving there. Some people leave requests for healing.

LAS POSADAS

In some parts of the United States, Latin Americans celebrate Las Posadas. This holiday lasts from December 16 to December 24. It is a reminder of the journey Joseph and Mary made. According to the Christian Bible, they traveled from Nazareth to Bethlehem. They were traveling to participate in a census. In Bethlehem, they searched for a safe place where Mary could give birth to Jesus.

Each evening during Las Posadas, a child dresses as an angel. They lead a procession through a town's streets.

Every year, a candlelit Las Posadas procession is held in Santa Fe, New Mexico. During the event, actors dress up as Mary and Joseph.

They stop at homes asking for a place to stay. The hosts serve refreshments. Parts of the Bible are read. People sing Christmas carols, too. Mass is held each day after the procession.

CHRISTMAS

Many Latin Americans have Christmas traditions, too. One happens shortly before Christmas Day. People build small cribs in their homes. Then they place a doll in the crib. It represents Jesus.

Colombian Americans gather around the manger. They pray and sing carols. They eat custard, fritters, and black cake. These traditions remind them of the countries they came from. Many Latin Americans pass their traditions on to their children.

Some Latin American Christmas celebrations involve star-shaped piñatas.

CHAPTER FOUR

LATIN AMERICANS TODAY

In 2023, there were about 65.2 million Latin Americans in the United States. Some states have more Latin Americans than others. In 2023, California and Texas had the largest Latin American populations.

Latin Americans have had to overcome many struggles in the United States. They have faced racism and injustice. But they have broken barriers to achieve great success. Many Latin Americans still face

US Representative Alexandria Ocasio-Cortez is the youngest Latina to ever serve in the US Congress. In 2024, she spoke at the Democratic National Convention in Chicago, Illinois.

challenges in the United States. But they have contributed greatly to US society.

CHANGEMAKERS, ARTISTS, AND ATHLETES

One notable Latin American is Cesar Chavez. He grew up poor. He never

In the 1960s, Cesar Chavez (center) led protests and boycotts focused on the rights of farm workers. One protest was centered around the US grape industry.

owned a car or a house. He never had a well-paying job, either. In the 1960s and 1970s, Chavez devoted his life to helping thousands of workers. He fought for them to receive fair wages and safe working conditions. He protested and led a historic march. This got the attention of the media and politicians. Chavez also fought against the unfair treatment of US farm workers. He founded the National Farm Workers Association.

Other Latin Americans have become successful government officials. Sonia Sotomayor broke boundaries in 2009. That year, she became the first Latina to serve on the US Supreme Court. She was also the third woman to serve on the court. Alexandria Ocasio-Cortez is a

US representative. She is from New York. Her mother was born in Puerto Rico. Her father was of Puerto Rican ancestry. In 2018, Ocasio-Cortez became a leading voice for Hispanic Americans in politics. Another Latin American politician is Marco Rubio. In 2005, he became the first Cuban American to serve as speaker of the Florida House of Representatives.

Latin Americans have contributed to entertainment, too. One example is Lin-Manuel Miranda. He is a composer and actor. He created and starred in the musical *Hamilton*. He also worked on several animated Disney films. These include *Moana* and *Encanto*. Miranda hopes to increase the number of Latin Americans in the industry. He also wants to tell more Latin

In 2018, Lin-Manuel Miranda was honored with a star on the Hollywood Walk of Fame in Los Angeles, California.

American stories. "I didn't see our stories being told so I wrote what was missing," he said.[5] Another Latin American entertainer is Jennifer Lopez. She is a singer and actress. Her parents were Puerto Rican.

Many well-known US athletes are Latin Americans, too. One is Roberto Clemente.

He was born in Puerto Rico. He was the first Latino inducted into the Baseball Hall of Fame. He was also known for his humanitarian efforts. In 1972, Clemente died in a plane crash. His plane was bringing supplies to Nicaragua. An earthquake had just struck the country.

Al Horford is a US basketball player. He is from the Dominican Republic. He acts as a role model for young Latin American athletes. Horford was a five-time NBA All-Star. He has played for the Atlanta Hawks and Boston Celtics. He works with communities and schools. Another Latin American basketball player is Eduardo Nájera. He was born in Mexico. He was the first Mexican-born player drafted to the NBA. He later worked as a scout for the Dallas Mavericks.

THE US-MEXICO BORDER

Since the 1970s, Mexican migrants have made up the largest percentage of people caught illegally crossing the US–Mexico border. Since 2000, lots of migrants have

Mexican migrants cross the US-Mexico border for a variety of reasons. Many seek jobs or better lives for their families.

come from Honduras, Guatemala, and El Salvador. Many people who cross the border want to claim **asylum**. They hope to escape poverty and crime in their home countries. In 2015, many Venezuelans began fleeing to the United States. They left Venezuela because of political turmoil there.

Today, many Americans believe the US immigration system is a problem. It can take years to become a US citizen. Courts are backed up with paperwork. Many white Americans believe the government should not allow more immigrants into the country. Some think the US health care system cannot handle more people. Some believe migrants are taking jobs from white Americans. Others believe migrants are the backbone of the United States. They fill many jobs that other people do not want. For example, some work in construction. They build new structures. Migrants often cross the border so their children can have better lives. Some have multiple jobs. Many do not have health insurance.

The US government has acknowledged that fixing the immigration system is crucial.

Latin Americans on Immigration

A 2024 survey asked people about immigration. It found that most Latin Americans in the United States believe more immigration judges should be hired. These judges could make quicker asylum decisions. Many Latin Americans would also like to make it easier for asylum seekers to legally work while waiting for decisions. Most Latin Americans do not support expanding the wall along the US–Mexico border. They say this would not fix the problem.

It is especially important for those who have waited decades for visas to enter the country. Many people in the United States want to legalize their status.

The issue of immigration has divided US political parties. Some believe illegal immigration should be stopped. They see it as a threat to the country. Others want to pass immigration laws. They say these will protect US security. They worry about drug trafficking and human trafficking. Both

In 2018, many Americans protested the separation of migrant parents and children at the US-Mexico border.

sides want a humane, fair solution. They understand the rights of migrants.

Americans continue to debate immigration issues. The issue has become a humanitarian and security crisis. Families risk their lives to come to the United States. Most people agree that immigration reform is needed for those who want to enter the country legally. Political parties will have to work together to find a solution.

Despite modern and past challenges, Latin Americans have made a place for themselves in the United States. They have shaped the country's history and culture. They have brought vibrant traditions. They have fought for change, too. Latin Americans continue to be an important part of the United States.

GLOSSARY

asylum

a form of protection that allows immigrants to stay in the United States if they are fleeing danger

heritage

practices and characteristics passed down from one generation to the next

immigrants

people who move to a different country

mass

a Christian religious service

origin

a person's or place's beginnings or birthplace

pilgrimage

a journey to a religiously significant place

regulated

controlled by rules or laws

resilience

the ability to recover from and adjust to challenges

rite

a ceremonial practice or tradition

SOURCE NOTES

CHAPTER ONE: THE HISTORY OF LATIN AMERICANS

1. Quoted in "'Cuidado!' The 158th Infantry 'Bushmasters' in the Pacific," *The National WWII Museum*, October 10, 2023. www.nationalww2museum.org.

CHAPTER TWO: CULTURES AND TRADITIONS

2. Quoted in Anita Snow, "Cinco de Mayo Celebrates Mexican Culture, Not Independence," *The Denver Post*, May 5, 2023. www.denverpost.com.

3. Quoted in Laura Rodriguez, "Thousands Attend Calle Ocho Music Festival in Miami's Little Havana," *NBC6*, March 12, 2023. www.nbcmiami.com.

CHAPTER THREE: RELIGIONS

4. Quoted in "Easter Pilgrimage to Chimayo," *The Pluralism Project: Harvard University*, n.d. https://pluralism.org.

CHAPTER FOUR: LATIN AMERICANS TODAY

5. Quoted in Marc Malkin, "Lin-Manuel Miranda Wrote 'In the Heights' Because Latinx Stories Were 'Missing' from Musical Theater," *Variety*, October 13, 2020. https://variety.com.

FOR FURTHER RESEARCH

BOOKS

Tammy Gagne, *Refugee and Immigrant Rights*. BrightPoint Press, 2025.

Monica Olivera, *Latin Americans in History: 15 Inspiring Latinas and Latinos You Should Know*. Rockridge Press, 2023.

Margeaux Weston and Sarosh Arif, *We are the United States*. Wide Eyed Editions, 2022.

INTERNET SOURCES

"Day of the Dead," *National Geographic Kids*, n.d. https://kids.nationalgeographic.com.

"Famous Latinos and Latinas," *National Museum of the American Latino*, n.d. https://latino.si.edu.

"Latin America," *Britannica Kids*, n.d. https://kids.britannica.com.

WEBSITES

Latin America Working Group
www.lawg.org

The Latin America Working Group is a nonprofit human rights organization that works to support Latin Americans in the United States and other countries. Its website provides information about human rights projects, immigration policies, and more.

Latino Americans Collection: PBS Learning Media
https://pbslearningmedia.org/collection/latino-americans

The Latino Americans collection from PBS Learning Media includes a variety of videos and online resources focused on Latin American history and culture.

National Museum of the American Latino
https://latino.si.edu

The National Museum of the American Latino is part of the Smithsonian in Washington, DC. It educates the public about Latin American history, art, and culture. The museum's website features virtual tours and information about exhibits.

INDEX

IMAGE CREDITS

Cover: © FG Trade Latin/iStockphoto
5: © FG Trade Latin/iStockphoto
7: © Victoria Ditkovsky/Shutterstock Images
9: © ezellhphotography/Shutterstock Images
11: © Salmonnegro-Stock/Shutterstock Images
12: © Roberto Galan/iStockphoto
15: © JennLShoots/Shutterstock Images
17: © Thiago Santos/iStockphoto
19: © Everett Collection/Shutterstock Images
20: © Everett Collection/Shutterstock Images
23: © Marjory Collins/Library of Congress
26: © Red Line Editorial
29: © Jorge Estrellado/Shutterstock Images
31: © Tatjana Baibakova/Shutterstock Images
34: © Betto Rodrigues/Shutterstock Images
37: © Juanmonino/iStockphoto
39: © Claudine Van Massenhove/Shutterstock Images
41: © JannHuizenga/iStockphoto
44: © Efrain Padro/Alamy
45: © Marcos Castillo/Shutterstock Images
47: © Maxim Elramsisy/Shutterstock Images
48: © Barry Sweet/AP Images
51: © Kathy Hutchins/Shutterstock Images
53: © Aaron Wells/Shutterstock Images
56: © KQW Photography/Shutterstock Images

ABOUT THE AUTHOR

Johannah Luza has been a freelance writer for many years. She currently writes educational books and children's books. She lives in Dallas, Texas.